WORSHIP GOD WITH YOUR WORK

SEE YOUR WORK AS A CALLING

This book is protected under the copyright laws of Ghana.

It may not be copied for commercial gain or profit, but permission will be granted if requested.

Quotations or occasional page copying is permitted and encouraged.

Copyright © 2014 Wester Communications.

Tel: 233243646650 Email: jadjei2@hotmail.com

ISBN-13: 978-1503060722

Unless otherwise stated, all scripture quotations are taken from the King James Version of the Bible.

PREFACE

"SEE YOUR WORK AS A CALLING"

Worship God with your job
Worship God with your vocation
Worship God with your career
Worship God with your profession
Worship God with your ministry

Whatever you do, work at it with all your heart, as working for the Lord, not for human masters. Col. 3:24.

For promotion cometh neither from the east, nor from the west, nor from the south. But God is the judge: he putteth down one, and setteth up another. Ps. 75:6-7

When men are cast down, then you shall say, There is lifting up; and he shall save the humble person. Job 22:29

The blessing of the LORD makes a person rich, and he adds no sorrow with it. Prov. 10:22

From Matthew 25:13-30, Jesus clearly shows through the parable of the Talents that the attitude of a Christian to work should be like that of the faithful servant- he was humble, holy, honest, dependable and benevolent.

[13] Watch therefore, for ye know neither the day nor the hour wherein the Son of man cometh.
[14] For the kingdom of heaven is as a man travelling into a far country, who called his own servants, and delivered unto them his goods.
[15] And unto one he gave five talents, to another two, and to another one; to every man according to his several ability; and straightway took his journey.
[16] Then he that had received the five talents went and traded with the same, and made them other five talents.

Worship God With your Work

17 And likewise he that had received two, he also gained other two.
18 But he that had received one went and digged in the earth, and hid his lord's money.
19 After a long time the lord of those servants cometh, and reckoneth with them.
20 And so he that had received five talents came and brought other five talents, saying, Lord, thou deliveredst unto me five talents: behold, I have gained beside them five talents more.
21 His lord said unto him, Well done, thou good and faithful servant: thou hast been faithful over a few things, I will make thee ruler over many things: enter thou into the joy of thy lord.
22 He also that had received two talents came and said, Lord, thou deliveredst unto me two talents: behold, I have gained two other talents beside them.
23 His lord said unto him, Well done, good and faithful servant; thou hast been faithful over a few things, I will make thee ruler over many things: enter thou into the joy of thy lord.
24 Then he which had received the one talent came and said, Lord, I knew thee that thou art an hard man, reaping where thou hast not sown, and gathering where thou hast not strawed:
25 And I was afraid, and went and hid thy talent in the earth: lo, there thou hast that is thine.
26 His lord answered and said unto him, Thou wicked and slothful servant, thou knewest that I reap where I sowed not, and gather where I have not strawed:
27 Thou oughtest therefore to have put my money to the exchangers, and then at my coming I should have received mine own with usury.
28 Take therefore the talent from him, and give it unto him which hath ten talents.
29 For unto every one that hath shall be given, and he shall have abundance: but from him that hath not shall be taken away even that which he hath.
30 And cast ye the unprofitable servant into outer darkness: there shall be weeping and gnashing of teeth.

HUMILITY

The servants were given a clear instruction as to what to do i.e trade with the talents and make profit for their master. Two of them were obedient, one refused to use his talent and it is important to note that those who obeyed did their work with alacrity and zeal. The parable says when they received the instruction they left <u>immediately</u> to work. They applied heavenly wisdom, which is humble, pure, sincere, fruitful, considerate and full of mercy. James 3:17.

The disobedient servant was selfish, and refused to make profit for His master. He applied earthly wisdom, which is bitterness, envy and selfish ambition and it is unspiritual and devilish. James 3:15.

The foremost lesson here is to fear God, love Him with all your heart and obey His commands.

HOLINESS
The servants were given talents according to their ability. Be strong in the might of the Lord.

"I can do all things through Christ who strengthens me". Phil. 4:13.

Be led by the Spirit, looking to the Holy Spirit for your daily strength means keeping your way pure by keeping the Word of God. Ps. 119:9.

The Holy Spirit is the source of our strength and He is the source of our uniqueness. Be unique and be what God has created you to be, operating within your capabilities and not outside your capabilities. Without Him we are nothing. Be pure and original. Jesus Christ was pure, no sin was found in Him. 1 Pt. 2:22.

HONESTY
The servants were faithful and truthful, they fulfilled their promises. They agreed to work and they fulfilled their promises except one. He should have told the master that he was not going to do the work, but he agreed and later buried his talent.

Worship God With your Work

The servants were expected to make profit, to be fruitful and they met the expectations of the master.

Be true to your calling and ensure you achieve your God-given assignment or divine purpose. The servants who made profit for their master were given rewards according the profit margin. To the one who made the highest profit, the master said

> "Well done, good and faithful servant; you were faithful over a few things, I will make you ruler over many things. Enter into the joy of your lord." Matt. 25:21.

DEPENDABILITY
Honesty makes you fulfill your promises but dependability makes you fulfill them to the letter.

For example, if I asked you to meet me on Wednesday at 5pm, in a white shirt and you came, but not at 5pm and not in a white shirt, you had been honest but not dependable. You promised to come and you honoured your promise but not according to the agreed specifications.

Dependability makes you do your work to specifications- pays attention to details and undertakes a meticulous delivery of assignments. This entails creativity and creativity means hard work- going the extra mile, spending time and resources on your work with full concentration. The obedient servants made 100% profit- excellent result!

Dependability depends on how much we depend on God. How much time we spend on the Word to know what God wants us to do and to do it exactly the way he wants it done.

Blessed is the man that walketh not in the counsel of the ungodly, nor standeth in the way of sinners, nor sitteth in the seat of the scornful. But his delight is in the law of the LORD; and in his law doth he meditate day and night. And he shall be like a tree planted by the rivers of water, that bringeth forth his fruit in his season; his leaf also shall not wither; and whatsoever he doeth shall prosper- Ps. 1:1-3

BENEVOLENCE
The disobedient servant was selfish and unwilling to help his master build up his business. He said his master wanted to reap where he had not sowed, so he refused to use his talent. Freely we have received and freely we must give. Every good and perfect gift comes from God and He gives them to us freely.

The disobedient servant was bitter, full of selfish ambition and envious of the profits to be made by the master. We must be selfless, compassionate and sensitive to the needs of others, not thinking of what gains we would make before helping people. We must be willing to work for the common good.

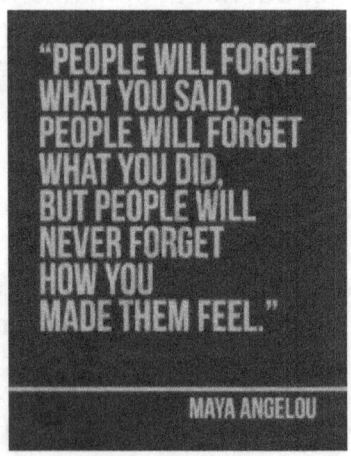

Contents

Corporate Culture.................................9

Leadership......................................14

Attitude..23

Communication...................................33

Values in the Workplace.........................43

1. Humility In The Workplace...................43
2. Holiness In The Workplace....................52
3. Honesty In The Workplace.....................58
4. Dependability In The Workplace...............62
5. Benevolence In The Workplace.................68

"Man is a spirit, has a soul and dwells in a body and any educational effort aimed at transforming human behavior without impacting the human spirit will hardly yield any positive results- the human spirit is the real person and not the soul nor the physical body."

CHAPTER 1

CORPORATE CULTURE

Introduction
Culture is the way living things behave, either individually(personal) or in a group(corporate). In the corporate environment, it is the embodiment(written or unwritten) of the policies and practices of the Company and the success or failure of the Company depends on the gap between company policy and company practice.

Corporate culture is the values and practices shared by the members of a group. Company Culture, therefore, is the shared values and practices of the company's employees.

Company culture is important because it can make or break your company. Companies with an adaptive culture that is aligned to their business goals routinely outperform their competitors. Some studies report the difference at 200% or more. To achieve results like this for your organization, you have to figure out what your culture is, decide what it should be, and move everyone toward the desired culture.

Corporate culture refers to the shared values, attitudes, standards, and beliefs that characterize members of an organization and define its nature. Corporate culture is (driven by) rooted in an organization's goals, strategies, structure, and approaches to labor.

It is an essential component in any business's ultimate success or failure. "[It] is an unwritten value-set that management communicates directly or indirectly that all employees know and work under," stated John O'Malley in *Birmingham Business Journal*. "It is the underlying soul and guiding force within an organization that creates attitude alliance, or employee loyalty. A winning corporate culture is the environmental keystone for maintaining the highest levels of employee satisfaction, customer loyalty, and profitability."

Culture can be a particularly important consideration for businesses. A healthy company culture may increase employees' commitment and productivity, while an unhealthy culture may inhibit a company's growth or even contribute to business failure.

Every company has a culture, though not every culture is beneficial in helping a company reach its goals. A healthy corporate culture is one in which employees are encouraged to work together to ensure the success of the overall business. Developing and maintaining a healthy corporate culture can be particularly problematic for entrepreneurs, as the authoritarian practices that helped establish a small business often must be exchanged for participatory management strategies that allow it to grow.

An Increasing Emphasis on Culture

Since the 1980s there has been an increasing emphasis on culture due to the transition from a manufacturing-based to a service-based economy, with the corresponding shift in emphasis from the quality of a material product to the quality of business relationships.

Corporate culture affects many areas of a firm's operations. One broad area of corporate culture involves corporate citizenship—the company's relationship to the larger environment. In this area, a company's culture helps determine its overall ethics and attitude toward public service.

A second broad area of corporate culture involves human resource management. A company's culture affects a variety of human resource policies and practices, including the nature of interaction between managers and employees, the responsiveness to diversity issues in the workplace, and the availability of flextime and telecommuting options, safety and training programs, and health and recreation facilities. In a smoothly functioning organization, all such policies and practices foster an internally consistent corporate culture.

Flextime is a variable work schedule, in contrast to traditional work arrangements requiring employees to work a standard 9 a.m. to 5 p.m. day. Under flextime, there is typically a core period (of approximately 50% of total working time / working day) of the day, when employees are expected to be at work (for example, between 11 a.m. and 3 p.m.), while the rest of the working day is "flexible time", in which employees can choose when they work, subject to achieving total daily, weekly or monthly hours in the region of what the employer expects, and subject to the necessary work being done

A flextime policy allows staff to determine when they will work, while a flexplace policy allows staff to determine where they will work. It allows employees to adopt their work hours to public transport schedules, to the schedules their children have, and that road traffic will be less congested, more spread out.

Flextime allows an employee to select the hours he or she will work. There are usually specified limits set by the employer. Employees on a flexible schedule may work a condensed work week or may work a regular work week. Those working a condensed week may work four ten hour days, rather than five eight hour days. Those who work a five day week may work hours other than the typical "nine to five."

Culture in Small Businesses

Many entrepreneurs, when they first start a new business, quite naturally tend to take on a great deal of responsibility themselves. As the company grows and adds employees, however, the authoritarian management style that the business owner used successfully in a very small company can become detrimental. Instead of attempting to retain control over all aspects of the business, the small business owner should strive to "get everybody else in the organization to do your job, while you create an environment so that they can do it."

In a healthy culture, employees view themselves as part of a team and gain satisfaction from helping the overall company succeed. When employees sense that they are contributing to a successful group effort, their level of commitment and productivity, and thus the quality of the company's products or services, are likely to improve.

In contrast, employees in an unhealthy culture tend to view themselves as individuals, distinct from the company, and focus upon their own needs. They only perform the most basic requirements of their jobs, and their main—and perhaps only—motivation is their paycheck.

Company cultures evolve and they change over time. As employees leave the company and replacements are hired the company culture will change. If it is a strong culture, it may not change much. However, since each new employee brings their own values and practices to the group the culture will change, at least a little. As the company matures from a startup to a more established company, the company culture will change. As the environment in which the company operates (the laws, regulations, business climate, etc.) changes, the company culture will also change.

These changes may be positive, or they may not. The changes in company culture may be intended, but often they are unintended. They may be major changes or minor ones. The company culture will change and it is important to be aware of the changes.

Since every company is different, there are many ways to develop a culture that works. Following are several main principles that small business owners should consider in order to create a healthy corporate culture:

1. Assess the Company Culture
There are many ways to assess your company culture. The easiest way to assess your company's culture is to look around. How do the employees act; what do they do? Look for common behaviors and visible symbols.

Listen. Listen to your employees, your suppliers, and your customers. Pay attention to what is written about your company, in print and online. These will also give you clues as to what your company's culture really is.

2. Determine the desired Company Culture
Before you can change the company culture, you have to decide what you want the company culture to look like in the future. Different companies in different industries will have different cultures. Look at what kind of a culture will work best for your organization in its desired future state. Review your mission, vision and values and make sure the company culture you are designing supports them.

CHAPTER 2

LEADERSHIP

Definition.
"Leadership is the art of getting someone else to do something you want done because he wants to do it." **Dwight D. Eisenhower**

Leadership can be put into two main categories i.e self leadership and corporate leadership. The former denotes how we ran our personal lives and the latter, how corporate bodies are ran, from vision casting, through implementation to evaluation. But the least common denominator of the two is that decisions have to be made, goals have to be set and people have to help achieve the goals.

Once you passed the age of being dictated to by your parents and you begin to take your own decisions, you become a leader. And because we all need people to help us do the things we want to do as leaders, we must know how to get people to do the things we want done , not through coercion nor because it is their duty, but because they want to do what we want them to do for us.

"Leadership is cause; everything else is effect." Cause is an emanation point. It is the source. It is the point in space where something originates. Effect is the receipt point. It receives a flow of some kind and is affected by it. The mark of a wise and mindful leader is his ability to extend an intention into space and become CAUSE.

Those whose actions come from integrity cause wonderful effects everywhere they go. An overwhelming majority of us are seeking to bring forth positive and wholesome actions and behaviors in this world. We desire to improve ourselves, our relationships and our businesses. We want to see a better world emerge from these troubling times.

One way to achieve this is to set your intention to be a wise and mindful leader in all aspects of your life. Truly great leaders seek to improve conditions in their sector or zone of influence, they share this common quality of causation. They are not the effect of their environment but they step outside it to be the cause of change.

Turn on your light
Turn on your light in the darkness. Be a better influence. Say it with your example and scarcely with your words. Be a witness and not a "preacher". Your life can preach a better sermon than your lips. People believe a sermon that is seen more than a sermon that is heard. Consistency in being a witness will drive the darkness away.

Be a witness to a better life. You do not have to convict people of their ways. That is the work of the Holy Spirit. They are already aware of their mistakes. You just have to be a witness to a better life and they will love to change. Let your light shine before men. Let them see your good works- your smile, love, kindness, mercy.

People do not care how much you know but want to know how much you care. Talk is cheap. People are watching your life. Anytime you react with someone, people are watching. What example do you set? Your life is your message and action speaks louder than words. Turning on your light will make a difference in people's lives. But it will also make a difference in your life because people will be kind and merciful to you, will love to be around you. "Let your light so shine before men, that they may see your good works, and glorify your Father which is in heaven." Matt. 5:16 and 2 Tim 2:19 says "they that name the name of Christ must depart from iniquity".

The greatest leadership role model of all time. "The more I read the Bible, the more evident it becomes that everything I have ever taught or written about effective leadership over the past 25 years, Jesus did to perfection. He is simply the greatest leadership role model of all time." Ken Blanchard

"And being found in fashion as a man, He humbled himself, and became obedient unto death, even the death of the cross.- Phil 2:8.

<u>Jesus washes the feet of His disciples.</u> **John 13:1-17**
Jesus Christ exhibited the highest level of leadership. He showed leadership by example-Jesus Washes His Disciples' Feet (John 13:1-17)

1. Now before the feast of the passover, when Jesus knew that his hour was come that he should depart out of this world unto the Father, having loved his own which were in the world, he loved them unto the end.
2 And supper being ended, the devil having now put into the heart of Judas Iscariot, Simon's son, to betray him;
3 Jesus knowing that the Father had given all things into his hands, and that he was come from God, and went to God;
4 He riseth from supper, and laid aside his garments; and took a towel, and girded himself.
5 After that he poureth water into a bason, and began to wash the disciples' feet, and to wipe them with the towel wherewith he was girded.
6 Then cometh he to Simon Peter: and Peter saith unto him, Lord, dost thou wash my feet?
7 Jesus answered and said unto him, What I do thou knowest not now; but thou shalt know hereafter.
8 Peter saith unto him, Thou shalt never wash my feet. Jesus answered him, If I wash thee not, thou hast no part with me.
9 Simon Peter saith unto him, Lord, not my feet only, but also my hands and my head.
10 Jesus saith to him, He that is washed needeth not save to wash his feet, but is clean every whit: and ye are clean, but not all.
11 For he knew who should betray him; therefore said he, Ye are not all clean.
12 So after he had washed their feet, and had taken his garments, and was set down again, he said unto them, Know ye what I have done to you?

Worship God With your Work

¹³ Ye call me Master and Lord: and ye say well; for so I am.
¹⁴ If I then, your Lord and Master, have washed your feet; ye also ought to wash one another's feet.
¹⁵ For I have given you an example, that ye should do as I have done to you.
¹⁶ Verily, verily, I say unto you, The servant is not greater than his lord; neither he that is sent greater than he that sent him.
¹⁷ If ye know these things, happy are ye if ye do them.

<u>What manner of man is this?</u> The Bible says of Jesus Christ, the best leader ever known,

"But the men marvelled, saying, What manner of man is this, that even the winds and the sea obey him!" Matt 8:27.

The true leader is a true worshiper and the true worshiper submits sincerely and willing to the true God- the Most High and Almighty God. SUBMIT TO THE CREATOR AND CREATION WILL SUBMIT TO YOU!

"And having in a readiness to revenge all disobedience, when your obedience is fulfilled." 2 Cor. 10:6.

To be ahead, to be a winner, to be a champion, to be a leader, you must first be led- and to be led you must be submissive. . This is an age-old principle.

<u>Man of great influence</u>
A leader can also be defined as "a person who influences a group of people towards the achievement of a goal".

Considering the influence Jesus has had in history and the number of followers He has had since His day, He would be the greatest leader who ever walked the earth in the chronicles of mankind.

How Jesus led was according to "the Spirit within Him," and qualities of leadership were apparent in all His works. Leadership is influence and leaders are defined by the number of faithful followers supporting them. In this case, Jesus has had more willing, loyal, and devoted followers than any man has ever had. Leadership is the ability to rally people together for one cause, and this is exactly what Jesus did, and has done through time.

But thinking about the issue critically, it should be an unfair exercise trying to compare other leaders to Jesus Christ, and that exercise may border on blasphemy- how can men be compared to God?

> "He that cometh from above is above all: he that is of the earth is earthly, and speaketh of the earth: he that cometh from heaven is above all." John 3:31.

How can you be a positive influence?
Leadership, whether on the personal or corporate level is a picture of the future of those who follow. Leadership should have a positive impact on those who follow and the question is "How can you be a positive influence?"

To impact our immediate environment and beyond, we must first be able to rise above our personal challenges or negative habits. This fact makes relational skills an indispensable part of leadership skills.

Habits are products of the heart and to change habits the heart must be changed. The effect is changed by changing the cause. The axe must be laid at the root and not at the leaves. To change the fruit the seed must be changed.

Changing human behaviour is not a moral problem. Bible says "Out of the heart are the issues of life.....troubles we have in life come from the heart – it is the ultimate decider of our actions. The unregenerated heart cannot obey the Word of God or walk in righteousness. Soft skills management is training acquired to retain effective relationships in our workplaces. But no matter how trained you are in soft skills management, if your heart is not changed you can hardly relate effectively.

We cannot solve a spiritual problem with moral program i.e soft skills management training. Man is a spirit, has a soul and dwells in a body and any educational effort aimed at transforming human behavior without impacting the human spirit will hardly yield any positive results- the human spirit is the real person and not the soul nor the physical body.

A moral program will at best produce a "a better you". However a spiritual program will produce "a new you" with a new attitude and the best and most effective communication skills.

Prevailing corporate culture begins at the top.
Entrepreneurs need to explain and share their vision of the company's future with their workers. "Let your vision for the company become their vision for the company," stated O'Malley. "A company without a vision is reactive in nature, and its management is seldom confident addressing competitive threats and stepping into the future." In addition, small business owners should be aware that their own behavior and attitudes set the standard for the entire workforce. Small business owners who set poor examples in areas such as lifestyle, dedication to quality, business or personal ethics, and dealings with others (customers, vendors, and employees) will almost certainly find their companies defined by such characteristics.

Treat all employees equally. Entrepreneurs should treat all employees equally. This does not mean that business owners can not bestow extra rewards on workers who excel, but it does mean that interactions with all employees should be based on a foundation of respect for them. One particular pitfall in this area for many small business owners is nepotism. Many small businesses are family-owned and operated. But bloodlines should be irrelevant in daily operations. "Successful

…businesses constantly place 'you are no different' expectations on family members they employ," noted O'Malley. "Doing otherwise quickly undermines employees' morale….Showing favoritism in the workplace is like swimming with sharks—you are destined to get bitten."

Hiring decisions should reflect desired corporate culture. The wise small business owner will hire workers who will treat clients and fellow employees well and dedicate themselves to mastering the tasks for which they are responsible. After all, "good attitude" is an essential component of any healthy corporate culture. But entrepreneurs and their managers also need to make sure that hiring decisions are not based upon ethnic, racial, or gender issues. Besides, businesses typically benefit from having a diverse workforce rather than one that is overly homogeneous.

Two-way communication is essential.

<u>Discuss problems.</u> Small business owners who discuss problems realistically with their workforce and enlist employees' help in solving them will likely be rewarded with a healthy internal environment. This can be an important asset, for once a participatory and engaging culture has been established, it can help propel a small business ahead of its competition.

<u>Do not ignore the warning signs.</u> Problems with the corporate culture can play a major role in small business failures. When employees only perform the tasks necessary to their own jobs, rather than putting out extra effort on behalf of the overall business, productivity declines and growth comes to a halt. Unfortunately, many entrepreneurs tend to ignore the developing cultures within their businesses until it is too late to make needed changes.

Some warning signs of trouble with the company culture:
-decreasing turnover

-difficulty in hiring talented people
-employees arriving at work and leaving for home right on time
-low attendance at company events
-a lack of honest communication and understanding of the company mission
-an "us-versus-them" mentality between employees and management
-declining quality and customer satisfaction.

A small business exhibiting one or more of these warning signs should consider whether the problems stem from the company culture. If so, the small business owner should take steps to improve the culture, including reaffirming the company's mission and goals and establishing a more open relationship with employees.

Leadership develops leaders

1. Why should leaders develop the leadership potential of those who report to them?

    a. It is very expensive to recruit and integrate new senior managers and leaders.
    b. Those in the team or the company, already understand the company culture
    c. They know the business environment
    d. They may have developed a strategic working relationship with key stakeholder groups.
    e. Your success as a leader is judged by your succession.

2. How do you unlock the leadership potential of those who report to you?

    a. Role model-they will learn most from your behaviours and actions and not your words

b. Release roles- challenge them to take on more responsibility. They will learn to be leaders faster by leading others.

c. Resist the urge- do not yield to the temptation of taking back control when you see that the going is becoming tough for the one you gave the responsibility to.

d. Support them:
i. know their strengths and weaknesses.

ii. know what drives them and where they want to go. Ask how you can help them.

iii. Prepare them, provide resources, set target lines, guidelines and deadlines.

iv. No-blame culture- support them when they fail. Deal with failure in a positive and supportive way. This encourages them to take risks.

v. Give both negative and positive feedback.

vi. Coach them- do not give all the answers. If you do that they will never think for themselves.

vii. Celebrate their successes.

CHAPTER 3

ATTITUDE

Attitudes are the established ways of responding to people and situations that we have learned, based on the beliefs, values and assumptions we hold. Attitudes become manifest through your behavior.

Your attitude determines your altitude. To succeed in anything you do you need attitude, skill and knowledge. But attitude is the most important. Research has established that to succeed in anything you do the right mix of these factors should be as follows:
- Attitude- 65%
- Skill- 25%
- Knowledge- 15%

It is attitude that determines how fast you achieve your goal or how well you acquire a skills or knowledge. Attitudes also provide a framework to solve the problem.

The only source of **happiness** – and unhappiness – comes from inside yourself.
Happiness is not something that comes to you. It is something you create now, today. Waiting for something to change in order to be happy is waiting to live **your life**. It is not what happens to you that counts. It is how you react to what happens to you. It is your attitude. When you adopt a positive attitude, life becomes a rewarding adventure instead of something to get through.

Attitude Drives Behavior
Attitudes drive behavior. If you want to succeed at anything you need to have the right mindset. Your body language is a result of your mental attitude. By choosing your attitude you get in that mood and send out a message that everyone understands, consciously or unconsciously.

"Almost always, you have a choice as to what attitude to adopt. There is nothing in any normal work situation that dictates you must react one way or another. If you feel angry about something that happens, for instance, that's how you choose to feel. Nothing in the event itself makes it absolutely necessary for you to feel that way. It is your choice. And since you do have a choice, most of the time you'll be better off if you choose to react in a positive rather than a negative way.

Nature | Nurture | Culture
Nurture personal culture to sync with corporate culture- conduct, rules and regulations of your organization.

Your nature influences your behavior and your behaviour represents your culture. Your personal culture may be at variance with that of your organization. Invariably workers fall short of the expectations of their organizations, regarding conduct, rules or regulations.

If you do not like the way you behave, watch your beliefs. Your beliefs define your values; your values form your mindset; and your mindset(attitude) influence your behavior (choices, decisions and goals).

Intellectual And Emotional Intelligence
Not many years ago, the intelligence quotient, or IQ, was seen as a strong indicator of the level of success one could attain in life. The standard IQ test measured raw intelligence, including abilities such as logic and reasoning skills, reading, writing, and analyzing. Research, however, soon proved that the IQ could not predict academic and professional performance as once had been thought. There was another element involved: emotional intelligence, also known as the EQ. Emotional intelligence measures one's understanding of emotions, the ability to empathize and work with others, and manage under stress. IQ seldom changes while EQ can change through self-discipline or a profound experience. Nonetheless, they function in tandem and are both important to personal

development and success.

If IQ defines how smart you are, EQ determines how you use that blessing. Individuals with high EQ's are better equipped to make use of their cognitive abilities. They are often chosen for advancement in their professions or volunteer experiences because they possess the ability to inspire people to action and to make others feel more confident. People with high IQ's but low EQ's sometimes sabotage themselves because they are unable to relate to their peers, cannot handle stress constructively, and find emotional connections difficult to maintain. Developing your EQ can help you access your innate intelligence and amplify your empathy, which can lead to career advancement and better relationships. Practice embracing your uniqueness and the uniqueness of others, expressing your feelings and interpreting those of your friends and family, and being decisive - all of which can help boost your EQ.

Experts say that a heightened EQ can bring happiness because it lets you focus on feelings as well as facts, whereas the IQ is concerned with logic. A strong EQ also makes you more able to access the benefits of your IQ because it takes both to build a successful career, strong relationships, and a fulfilling life.

Soft Skills
Soft skills is a term often associated with a person's "EQ" (Emotional Intelligence Quotient), the cluster of personality traits, social graces, communication, personal habits, friendliness etc..

Soft skills complement hard skills which are the occupational requirements of a job and many other activities. They are related to feelings, emotions, insight or inner knowing. Personal habits and traits such as dependability and conscientiousness can yield significant return on a person's work or the work of an organization. Research has shown that

the most successful or leading organizations in the world today acknowledge the vital role personal attitude or character plays in their success and that has led to a rise in the value of soft skills at the work place. Standard qualification for the selection of employees or promotion in the work place, is not based only on hard skills, but also on soft skills.
Soft skills are behavioral competences, interpersonal skills or people skills, including proficiencies such as:
- good communication skills
- conflict resolution and negotiation
- strategic thinking
- team building
- influencing skills
- work ethic
- time management
- problem solving skills

Soft skills denotes the way you relate with people, the way you treat people, as an individual or as a cooperate entity. Hard Skills is about intellectual intelligence and Soft Skills is about emotional intelligence-how you relate with people; being sensitive to the emotional needs of people; your behaviour, character etc. Soft Skills management is very vital in leadership, whether personal or corperate because it creates and enhances effective relationships. Soft skills management will increase the profit margin of your company and create loyal customers for you.

Personal attributes
Soft skills are personal attributes that enable someone to interact effectively and harmoniously with other people. Relating effectively and harmoniously with people requires certain skills e.g. negotiation, communication, time management etc and it is central to building a lasting relationship with people in general, including customers or clients. Soft skills management alias "people skills" or interpersonal skills, is basically how to relate with people. You can be thought how to relate with people but it has to be in

Worship God With your Work

you to do it. It must be a personal attribute. You must have the intrinsic qualities to do it. You have to be predisposed to it to be able to do it. Knowledge is not enough- you need power to do it and that power comes from God.

Morality- being good.
Morality is knowledge of good and evil. It denotes how we the creatures relate with one another and spirituality is about how we the creatures relate with our Creator. If you love God then you can love the people around you and be good to them. Right relationship with God automatically translates into a right relationship with your neighbour. So scripture declares "If a man says, I love God, and hates his brother, he is a liar: for he that loves not his brother whom he has seen, how can he love God whom he has not seen?"1 John 4:20.

Love for your neighbor is driven by your love for God. That is why in the commandments of Jesus Christ, love for God came before love for neighbor:

"'Love the Lord your God with all your heart and with all your soul and with all your mind.' 38 This is the first and greatest commandment. 39 And the second is like it: 'Love your neighbor as yourself'" Matt 22:37-39.

Love for neighbor is underpinned by what has come to be known as the Golden rule

"Therefore all things whatsoever ye would that men should do to you, do ye even so to them"- Matt 7:12

Soft Skills- The Next Level

Spiritual issue
Intellectual and emotional intelligence are not enough for professional success. Man is a spirit, has a soul and dwells in a body and no worker can give off his best if whatever training he benefits from, does not impact his spirit. A worker may be

both intellectually and emotionally intelligent but if he lacks spiritual intelligence, his capacity to relate in the work place will not be effective. Such a person may know what to do but invariably falls short of how to do it- attitude, and as they say attitude is everything.

Hitherto, soft skills have been treated as a moral issue but we cannot solve a spiritual problem with a program of moral improvement. Soft skills management requires a program that brings spiritual transformation to a life.

It is common knowledge how we are often let down by our emotions. Have you ever said "I was surprised by his behaviour" and sometimes not only you but the one in question himself is shocked by his own behaviour? Yes that is the old or Adamic nature for you! So unpredictable- shows up when least expected. Many a time when we least expect, our behaviour gives us away because we failed to behave the way we know to be right and the way people know to be right and the reason is that the unregenerated person has no control over his emotions. The flesh wants to do what it wants to do, when it wants to do it and the unregenerated person has no control at all.

In order for soft skills training to be effective, the training must be targeted at the heart or the human spirit and not the soul(the intellect and the emotions). Soft skills is about behavior and behavior influenced by mindset or attitude. So to ensure that we are not taken by surprise to do what we do not want to do and regret later we need to focus on our mindsets and to get the right mindset we need to check our values and to ensure we have the right values we need to have the right beliefs.

This is because your beliefs define your values; your values form your mindset; and your mindset(attitude) influences your behavior (choices, decisions and goals). Believe in the Word of God and let it be the basis for your values, mindset and behaviour.

Talent is not enough

Fruitfulness depends on attitude, skills and knowledge. But attitude is the most important of the three factors according to research as it contributes 65% to your success, skill 25% and knowledge 10% in that order.

You know what to do-intellectual intelligence. How you do what you do is emotional intelligence-being sensitive to the emotions of people and making people happy through kind speeches and actions.

Here is where the problem lies. You need a higher level of empowerment-spiritual intelligence. Are you finding the rules and regulations in your organization too cumbersome to cope with? Your nature- how you have been nurtured through home discipline and personal experiences is at variance with the expectations of your organization, regarding discipline-obeying its rules and regulations. Your nature has to be renurtured to conform to the corporate culture. Personal culture affects corporate culture-how people see the organization or the image of the organization. There should not be any gaps between policy and practice, regarding what the rules and regulations are and the behavior of staff. The two should be in sync.

Behaviour is how one reacts under various circumstances and the way we react to a situation depends on our character, mindset or attitude.

Behavior is not conduct. Conduct is actionary. Behavior is reactionary. Reaction does not involve reasoning. What is in you-character, mindset or attitude, is what comes out. You cannot give out what you do not have.

Issues to be addressed

Attitude is your mindset and it drives your behavior. Attitude affects your goals, choices and decisions- things you choose to do.

However all these are influenced by your values because values form your mindset or attitude. For example if humility is a value you cherish, it becomes your mindset to strive to be humble in all you do- in your conversation and conduct. And because humility is a godly attitude, it is more than capable to get you into the good books of people.

If you are not humble, you may pretend but your real character will definitely show up one day- one cannot pretend for long.

"A good tree cannot bring forth evil fruit; neither can a corrupt tree bring forth good fruit. Every tree that bringeth not forth good fruit is hewn down, and cast into the fire"- Matt 7:18-19

Soft skills are behavioral competences, interpersonal skills or people skills, including proficiencies such as:
- good communication skills
- conflict resolution and negotiation
- strategic thinking
- team building
- influencing skills
- work ethic
- time management
- problem solving skills

You can have all these skills, complemented by your hard skills, but without a godly attitude you cannot be successful professionally. Character is the bedrock of all good relationships and for that godly character is central to every sustainable relationship.

Fruitfulness entails knowing God's will and doing it. Doing God's will or godliness, is the ability to live like Jesus Christ

Worship God With your Work

lived and every believer has this ability. In John 1:12 the Bible says

"But as many as received him, to them gave he power to become the sons of God, even to them that believe on his name."

As children and citizens of God's kingdom our utmost duty is to know and practice the lifestyle and culture of the kingdom, which is righteousness.

"Seek first the kingdom of God, and his righteousness; and all these things shall be added unto you"- Matt 6:33.

God had planned that we would delight in Him and please Him in whatever we do.

We would know the commands of the king and be obedient citizens of the kingdom. He has written His laws on our hearts and shared His love abroad in our hearts. For He has given us the gift of righteousness, whereby we please Him naturally without any difficulty. This is the result of an intimate loving relationship with the King of Kings, Jesus Christ. For we are able to obey Him because perfect love casts out all fear- perfect love leads to trust and trust leads to obedience.

"If you love me, keep my commands" John 14:15.

When the Principle is applied by obeying the commandments of Jesus Christ.

"Love the Lord your God with all your heart and with all your soul and with all your mind.[38] This is the first and greatest commandment. [39] And the second is like it: 'Love your neighbor as yourself'" Matt 22:37-39.

Worship God With your Work

If you obey the commands of Christ, your life will change. You will not do different things but will do things differently. You will still be ordinary but do extra ordinary things.

CHAPTER 4

COMMUNICATION IN THE WORKPLACE

To communicate means to convey an information and receive a feedback.
Types Of Communication- Verbal And Body Language.

Body Language.
This is prevalent in more traditional societies in the world, as opposed to modern ones like America, where verbal communication prevails.

Sign of respect-put the hands behind the back when being talked to; bow when greeting.

Sign of petition- raise one palm and put it in the other repeatedly.

Sign of paying attention-looking into the eyes of the speaker.

Sign of disinterest- pretending to be busy whilst being talked to.

Verbal Language.

Words are carriers. When we speak, whatever we say either go to release the potential of the listener or to limit his potential. Words either empower or dispower(disable).

Words are creative. God's word is powerful and filled with faith. Words were the instruments by which God created all things. Hebrews 11:3- Through faith we understand that the worlds were framed by the Word of God…

Nine times the words, "And God said" appears in Genesis chapter one. Each time God spoke something was created, formed, or made. The worlds came into being, were beautifully coordinated, and now exist by the command of God.

By the Word of the Lord were the heavens made; and all the host of them by the breath of His mouth…For He spake, and it was done; He commanded, and it stood fast. Psalms 33:6-9

Thou has established the earth and it abideth. They continue this day according to thine ordinance; for all are thy servants. Psalms 119:89-91

Upholding all things by the Word of His power. Hebrews 1:3

Upholding and maintaining and guiding and propelling the universe by His mighty word of power. Hebrews 1:3 Amp.

God's word is full of power Luke 1:37 (ASV). For no word from God shall be void of power. God's word is full of power, creative energy, and life. When God created the universe, He used His word like a carpenter uses his hammer. God builds with His word. When God speaks, His word carries out His every bidding. His word is controlling this universe.

So will the words that come out of my mouth not come back empty-handed. They'll do the work I sent them to do, they'll complete the assignment I gave them. Isaiah 55:11MSG

Creation was established by God's Words and responded to the words spoken by Jesus. With faith filled words Jesus calmed the raging sea. With faith filled words Jesus raised the widow's son. With faith filled words Jesus called Lazarus from the tomb. Jesus spoke creative words to the man with the withered hand. Jesus spoke healthy words to the woman with the spirit of infirmity. To the paralytic Jesus' words were,

"Take up thy bed". In Matthew 8:5-13,

Worship God With your Work

The centurion knowing the authority and power of Jesus' words proclaimed, "Speak the Word only and my servant shall be healed".

He whom God hath sent speaketh the Words of God... John 3:34

I speak to the world those things which I have heard of Him...But as My Father hath taught Me, I speak these things. John 8:26, 28

For I have not spoken of myself but the Father which sent Me, He gave Me commandment what I should say and what I should speak. John 12:49-50.

Throughout the life and ministry of Jesus, He only spoke the creative, life giving words of His Father. People saw and recognized the power and authority of Jesus' word.

And they were astonished at His doctrine for His Word was with power. Luke 4:32

The power of God's Word on your lips.
And God said, Let Us make man in Our image, after Our likeness... Genesis 1:26-28

God made us in His image so that we could act like Him. To be a Christian is to be Christ like.

Be ye therefore followers (imitating, walking like, talking like, acting like) God. Ephesians 5:1

Thou has made him (man) a little lower than God and did set man over the works of Thy hands. Psalms 8:5.

His word expressed through scripture is so much more than a manual. The very breath of God is on it and in it. Through scripture (the written word) I can come to Jesus (the living word). As I hear the living word speak by the Spirit through scripture and in scriptural ways (see my Hearing God series) things change within me. Stuff I didn't have before appears.

My motives get transformed. My identity gets formed. God's word creates. If I'm a new creation (2Cor 5:17), then this is exactly what I should expect God's word to do. It's what I need. It's what God does in me through his word.

Communication of the team leader -Vision Casting
"YOU DON'T KNOW HOW STRONG YOU ARE UNTILL BEING STRONG IS THE ONLY CHOICE" This quote is similar to what we say locally, "Where there is a will, there is a way" or "you can get it if you really want". Furthermore it can be clearer, imagining jumping over a wall in your house to escape being killed by a lion, an action you could not have taken under normal circumstances.

Operating at the maximum potential is a function of inner motivation, rather than external benefits like money or material benefits. Empirical evidence shows that a worker is more fulfilled contributing to corporate success by playing his role successfully than the remuneration he receives.

Management sets the pace for the success of the company. The way employees treat the Company and relate with customers depends on how they are treated by management. Creating expectations and empowering people to follow them by following them yourself. Be good in how you relate with your employees- from communication to remuneration.

The team leader challenges team members, enables and encourages them. Challenge the team by casting or communicating the vision effectively, enable them by leading the way and encourage them to line up.

When you are casting vision, ensure the vision is:

Clear- Clarity around a vision is imperative. As the communicator, you have to be clear about your understanding of it. This is why writing the vision is also imperative. This written documentation is what you will return to again and again. Through a meticulous process, you learn how to communicate the vision clearly. When the vision is clear to you, you are more able to clearly communicate it to others.

Whether you are communicating the vision of the church or the vision for a new initiative, ensure you do so with absolute clarity. It is not about how much you share, but you must share enough for people to have complete clarity. Therefore, when you cast vision to God's people, be sure it is clear.

Concrete- I think having a concrete vision means that you have a vision that is real and tangible. It is not about using language that no one understands or trying to impress others with great and extensive content. It is a vision that people can touch, feel, and become engaged in personally.

Pastors seem to spiritualize issues. We cannot always spiritualize an initiative and have it received by the people. We have to know God wants us to do it, even have it confirmed from His Word; however, we have to communicate the vision in a believable and tangible manner. Therefore, when casting a vision, be clear and concrete.

Concise- In today's world it is really true: less is more. This is especially true when we cast a vision. It needs to be concise. It needs to be brief, free of too many details.

Yes, you have to go deep and comprehend the details so you know you understand the vision; however, when you cast it before others, they just need to know the work is already done. You need to be on top of it, but remember you are breaking it down, not only so others can grasp it, but also for them to be able to communicate it to others. I will state it again: It is not about how much you share, but share enough for the people to have complete clarity.

Therefore, when casting vision, be clear, concrete, and concise.

Compelling- A compelling vision moves the people to action. As a servant-leader, you are God's instrument to rally the people to a better future. You are there to lead them into a future where they would not go on their own. The vision has to be clear enough for them to understand, concrete enough for them to believe it is real, concise enough for them to communicate, and compelling enough for them to own personally and enthusiastically.

As the communicator of the vision, do your very best to be strong, believable, and capable of moving people into owning the vision enthusiastically. If the vision is going to capture their imagination and heart, moving them into the vision personally and enthusiastically, then the vision must be compelling.

Leadership is a privilege
Leadership is such a privilege because you are able to cast vision to others. Steward this entrustment well. Do not get lost in it. Enjoy it. You have the privilege to take them where you believe God wants to go. Therefore, be clear. Be concrete. Be concise. Be compelling.

The Call for Communication
In your hearts honor Christ the Lord as holy, always being prepared to make a defense to anyone who asks you for a reason for the hope that is in you; yet do it with gentleness and respect, having a good conscience, so that, when you are slandered, those who revile your good behavior in Christ may be put to shame. (1Pt. 3:15-16 ESV).

In other words we should not beat people over the head with the truth, but rather we should communicate with "gentleness" and "respect".

Leadership Protocol For Communication
Remember this, my dear brothers and sisters:

Worship God With your Work

Everyone should be quick to listen, slow to speak, and should not get angry easily. An angry person doesn't do what God approves of. (Jas 1:19-20).

A leader should be ever ready to hear the hearts and burdens of other people –first. Then he should respond without anger.

Let no corrupting talk come out of your mouths, but only such as is good for building up, as fits the occasion, that it may give grace to those who hear. (Eph 4:29 ESV).

A leader should never speak things that are indecent, but rather they should speak in context for the purpose of building-up the listeners.

Put away from you crooked speech, and put devious talk far from you. (Pro 4:24 ESV).

A leader should always be honest and not play games with words.

Let your speech always be gracious, seasoned with salt, so that you may know how you ought to answer each person. (Col 4:6 ESV).

Salt is a preservative and a wonderful source of flavor. Ministers should answer people in a way preserves their conversation, seasons their thoughts, and that suits the personality of those who hear.

In Revelation chapters 2-3 we see that Jesus first praised the churches before he admonished them. This is a powerful approach to correction. Opening statements of reproof should be seasoned with a word of encouragement or praise if at all possible. Doing so will greatly increase the chances of people listening.

a. Remember this, my dear brothers and sisters: Everyone should be quick to listen, slow to speak, and should not get angry easily. An angry person doesn't do what God approves of. (Jas 1:19-20).

b. Let no corrupting talk come out of your mouths, but only such as is good for building up, as fits the occasion, that it may give grace to those who hear. (Eph 4:29 ESV).

c. Put away from you crooked speech, and put devious talk far from you. (Pro 4:24 ESV).

    i) QUICK TO LISTEN (Jas 1:19-20.
    ii) SLOW TO SPEAK   "
    iii) SLOW TO ANGER   "
    iv) BUILD UP LISTENERS (Eph 4:29 ESV).
    v) HONEST SPEECH. (Prov. 4:24 ESV).
    vi) GRACIOUS SPEECH. (Col 4:6 ESV).
    vii) PRAISE BEFORE REPROOF (Revels. chapters 2-3)

Let your speech at all times be gracious (pleasant and winsome), seasoned [as it were] with salt, [so that you may never be at a loss] to know how you ought to answer anyone [who puts a question to you]. Colossians 4: 6

By long forbearance and calmness of spirit a judge or ruler is persuaded, and soft speech breaks down the most bonelike resistance. Proverbs 25: 15

He who goes about as a talebearer reveals secrets; therefore associate not with him who talks too freely. Proverbs 20: 19

A man has joy in making an apt answer, and a word spoken at the right moment--how good it is! Proverbs 15: 23

For we all often stumble and fall and offend in many things. And if anyone does not offend in speech [never says the wrong things], he is a fully developed character and a perfect man, able to control his whole body and to curb his entire nature. James 3: 2

Worship God With your Work

My mouth shall speak the praise of the Lord; and let all flesh bless (affectionately and gratefully praise) His holy name forever and ever. Psalm 145: 21

These are the things that you shall do: speak every man the truth with his neighbor; render the truth and pronounce the judgment or verdict that makes for peace in [the courts at] your gates. Zechariah 8: 16

So Eli said to Samuel, Go, lie down. And if He calls you, you shall say, Speak, Lord, for Your servant is listening. So Samuel went and lay down in his place. 1 Samuel 3: 9

Right and just lips are the delight of a king, and he loves him who speaks what is right. Proverbs 16: 13

The thoughts of the wicked are shamefully vile and exceedingly offensive to the Lord, but the words of the pure are pleasing words to Him. Proverbs 15: 26

He who guards his mouth keeps his life, but he who opens wide his lips comes to ruin. Proverbs 13: 3

But I tell you, on the day of judgment men will have to give account for every idle (inoperative, nonworking) word they speak. For by your words you will be justified and acquitted, and by your words you will be condemned and sentenced. Matthew 12: 36-37

[The Servant of God says] The Lord God has given Me the tongue of a disciple and of one who is taught, that I should know how to speak a word in season to him who is weary. He wakens Me morning by morning, He wakens My ear to hear as a disciple [as one who is taught]. Isaiah 50: 4

A soft answer turns away wrath, but grievous words stir up anger. Proverbs 15: 1

The tongue of the wise utters knowledge rightly, but the mouth of the [self-confident] fool pours out folly. Proverbs 15: 2

Worship God With your Work

A gentle tongue [with its healing power] is a tree of life, but willful contrariness in it breaks down the spirit. Proverbs 15: 4

And let your instruction be sound and fit and wise and wholesome, vigorous and irrefutable and above censure, so that the opponent may be put to shame, finding nothing discrediting or evil to say about us. Titus 2: 8

To slander or abuse or speak evil of no one, to avoid being contentious, to be forbearing (yielding, gentle, and conciliatory), and to show unqualified courtesy toward everybody. Titus 3: 2

So speak and so act as [people should] who are to be judged under the law of liberty [the moral instruction given by Christ, especially about love]. James 2: 12

*But the human tongue can be tamed by no man. It is a restless (undisciplined, irreconcilable) evil, full of deadly poison. With it we bless the Lord and Father, and with it we curse men who were made in God's likeness!
James 3: 8-9*

A man's [moral] self shall be filled with the fruit of his mouth; and with the consequence of his words he must be satisfied [whether good or evil]. Proverbs 18: 20

Death and life are in the power of the tongue, and they who indulge in it shall eat the fruit of it [for death or life]. Proverbs 18: 21

*Therefore encourage (admonish, exhort) one another and edify (strengthen and build up) one another, just as you are doing.
1 Thessalonians 5:11*

Set a guard, O Lord, before my mouth; keep watch at the door of my lips. Psalm 141:3

VALUES IN THE WORKPLACE

1. Humility In The Workplace

Proverbs 22:4 promises that, "Humility and the fear of the Lord bring wealth and honor and life." Maintaining a lifestyle of biblical humility brings glory to God, as well as "wealth and honor" to you. James 4:10 says,

"Humble yourselves before the Lord, and he will lift you up."

Biblical humility is simply recognizing your dependence on God. Andrew Murray in his classic book, Humility, says, "Humility is the highest virtue of a human being. In fact, it is the root of every virtue."

If you are humble, you are in very good company.
Numbers 12:3 proclaims,
"Now Moses was a very humble man, more humble than anyone else on the face of the earth."

Moses was a man of historic achievement. The books of Exodus, Leviticus, Numbers and Deuteronomy record the amazing things God did through him. Moses was a "very humble" man yet a great man—his life demonstrates that great humility goes hand-in-hand with great accomplishment.

Humility is never about denying your talents or successes. Humble people are simply more God-centered and other-people-centered than they are self-centered.

Some in the world turn the definition of humility upside down, and make it synonymous with weakness, inferiority, and even self-abasement. Don't believe them. They do not understand humility, but we will love them just the same.

Worship God With your Work

Humility exalts God, while pride, the opposite of humility, exalts self.
Consider Luke 14 which records Jesus' parable concerning the humble. The setting of the parable is a Sabbath dinner at the home of a prominent Pharisee. The Pharisee and his guests were the movers and shakers of the community. They were affluent, well-educated, and influential—the social and religious elites of their time.

Jesus seized the opportunity and his message to them is recorded in Luke 14:7-10:
When he [Jesus] noticed how the guests picked the places of honor at the table, he told them this parable: "When someone invites you to a wedding feast, do not take the place of honor, for a person more distinguished than you may have been invited. If so, the host who invited both of you will come and say to you, 'Give this man your seat.' Then, humiliated, you will have to take the least important place. But when you are invited, take the lowest place, so that when your host comes, he will say to you, 'Friend, move up to a better place.' Then you will be honored in the presence of all your fellow guests."
This parable has many applications, but when applied to the workplace the issue is self-exaltation versus humility. The elites in the story scrambled for the "place of honor" but they were moved to a lower place by the "host." The "host" in this parable represents God. It is God who will move you, the humble person, "to a better place" where you "will be honored in the presence of all your fellow guests."

Luke 14:11 expresses Jesus' key point:
"For everyone who exalts himself will be humbled, and he who humbles himself will be exalted."

Cultivate a lifestyle of humility and make it a part of your witness to others. Use your talents and pursue success while avoiding the worldly practice of self-exaltation.

Demonstrating the value

'Humility' is a widely understood word. It's not one of those words people will pause to look up the meaning for. Generally, people love the thought of humility. It's one of those 'good' values we strive for; one we admire. Yes, most people feel they know what it means to be humble.

Demonstrating it however, is a whole other matter.
For instance, a person distracted by their Blackberry or cell phone, unable to focus on the conversation you are having with them face to face, is so filled with self-importance, they cannot possibly claim to be humble. Humility is the lack of self-importance, is it not?

The person who impatiently shakes their head as you explain a new idea you are presenting to them, finally breaking in to say, "We've tried that here before, and it just doesn't work," cannot claim to be humble. Humility is being open-minded, and realizing that no matter how long you've been around, you couldn't possibly have experienced everything there is to experience, right?

Then there's the person who just got a promotion, and the first purchase order they write is for new business cards, despite the fact that the have a box left of the old ones with the same mailing address, email address, and phone numbers. Never mind that they mostly attach v-cards electronically these days, and that's why the old box lasted so long.

In new product development, there's a discussion going on about complaints customers have with existing products, and someone says, "Well, they wouldn't have that problem if they followed the instructions in the first place." That can't possibly be humility, when we stop listening to what our customers are asking for, and assume they just don't 'get it,' right?

If some of our common behaviors in workplaces are an indication, we don't understand humility very much at all.

Those who are humble, feel the rest of us are pretty interesting. Those with humility have a genuine desire to discover what other people can offer. They are intrigued by how others think, and how others feel differently from them.

We can be confident, and we can be self-assured; humility does not call for us to be meek, or consider ourselves lower in stature. We do not require less of ourselves, and we take our role and our responsibilities seriously.

However what humility does, is create a sort of receptacle of acceptance in us, so we are open to being filled with the knowledge and opinions of others. Humility is a kind of hunger for more abundance. The greater our humility, the greater our fascination with the world around us, and the more we learn.

To have inner drive, to want to be successful is a good thing. I do believe that part of humility is believing in those possibilities which presently may be larger than life for you. However humility also speaks to the demeanor and attitude we must have as we seek our success, so that our inner drive and desires are in balance with our composure, and our conduct with those who interact with us. After all, they could factor into being a big part of the success we eventually will enjoy.

One of the best definitions I have ever heard for humility came from one of my employees when I was still in corporate management. Short and sweet, it's one I have never forgotten. He was talking about a new supervisor we'd recently hired into the department, explaining how she listened to everyone on staff in such a great way. Like they mattered. Like everything they did and said mattered. He had said she seemed very humble to him because as she demonstrated it, "Humility is an act of courtesy."

We were not put on this earth alone. Frankly, others have to live with us, and our own practice of open-minded, fill-me-up humility can make it a much more interesting and pleasant experience for all of us.

Humility is key to leadership in the workplace

First, we need to establish a few things. Humility is not hospitality, courtesy, or a kind and friendly demeanour. Humility has nothing to do with being meek, weak or indecisive.

Perhaps more surprising, it does not entail shunning publicity. Organisations need people who understand marketing, including self-marketing, to flourish and prosper.
How can organisations cultivate humility in their leadership ranks?
How would that goal take shape in a formal leadership development program?

As a starting point, we suggest a curriculum designed around six basic principles. If you're a developing leader, you should be taught to:

Know what you don't know. Resist "master of the universe" impulses. You may excel in an area but as a leader you are, by definition, a generalist. Rely on those who have relevant qualification and expertise. Know when to defer and delegate.

Resist falling for your own publicity. Whether we're writing a press release or a self-appraisal, we all put the best spin on our successes – and then, conveniently, forget that the reality wasn't as flawless. Drinking in the glory of a triumph can be energising. Too big a drink is intoxicating. It blurs vision and impairs judgment.

Never underestimate the competition. You may be brilliant, ambitious and audacious. However, the world is filled with other hard-working, high-IQ and creative professionals. Don't kid yourself and assume that they and their innovations aren't a serious threat.

Embrace and promote a spirit of service. Employees quickly figure out which leaders are dedicated to helping them succeed and which are scrambling for personal success at their expense. Customers do so, too.

Listen, even (no, especially) to the weird ideas. People usually only listen to what someone else is saying when they are not confident their own ideas are – or will be – better than someone else's ideas. However, there is ample evidence that you should pay attention: the most imaginative and valuable ideas tend to come from left field, from some associate who seems a little offbeat and may not hold an exalted position in the organization.

Be passionately curious. Constantly welcome and seek out knowledge, and insist on curiosity from those around you. Research has found links between curiosity and many positive leadership attributes, including emotional and social intelligence. Take it from Einstein. "I have no special talent," he claimed. "I am only passionately curious."

We can't imagine that an individual exposed to the six principles above and encouraged to take them to heart could become anything but a better leader.

Demonstrating the attitude.
Humility is not about humiliation. Humility is about truth, the truth inherent in the statement, "God is God and I am not." Humility is about attitude, the attitude that drives how we interact with our fellow workers. It is about acknowledging God as whole and perfect and being aware of our individual imperfection and limitations.

It is not about abjectly denying our capabilities and worthiness. It is about fully and freely accepting the worth of all others, whilst acknowledging our need to continue to strive for integrity and perfection. It is about recognizing that all in the workplace have gifts of knowledge, talent, and/or capabilities, and they are all different. We acknowledge and value that other people have strengths which we do not have. Being humble is about utilizing our gifts AND the gifts of all co-workers, seeking their contribution to the work at hand and doing so with appreciation and thankfulness.

Humility at work also takes into account the contributions we as individuals and as a workplace can make to the common good of our communities. Profit and/or recognition are not sought directly, at all costs, but are allowed to arise from the provision of quality products and services, of just and caring attention to the needs of employees, customers, and the community.

The CEO of one of the nation's leading financial companies, one not embroiled in the "too big to fail" disasters of recent times, tells the story of one of the turning point moments in his leadership development. It was the final exam for a course in leadership. It consisted of one question, "Remember the janitorial worker who set up the lecture hall and cleaned up after class. What was her name?"

Seeking out and seeking to learn from all who are engaged in our workplace does two things in my opinion. One, we are likely to learn something about our work that we did not previously know; and two, we help that person Understand that they are part of the enterprise that we are about. Honestly listening to and learning from those we work with and for requires setting aside our egos; that is humility.

This can be particularly true in evaluations. When egos are at the fore, defense mechanism leap to any critical comment. When humility is present, when the ego is set aside, learning and growth can take place. When humble persons give evaluations, they begin with the possibility that there may be information that, if known, could change their judgment. So they present the information underlying their judgment as well as the reasoning that led to their judgment. They actually seek to discuss the information and the reasoning with the person being evaluated. They seek to learn what they do not know.

This same attitude is present in those who receive evaluations with humility. They seek to learn that which they do not know, essentially the information and reasoning that led the evaluator to his/her conclusions. It is not about ego but about development and growth.

Humility should flow from our understanding that God created all of us, our world, and our universe. We humans are brothers and sisters in his creation. We are all his children, none more so than another. In that equality of creation, we are none of us more worthy than another. We owe respect and courtesy to our co-workers, our customers, our communities, and, lastly, to ourselves.

When we put ourselves last, being a servant to others, then we act out of humility, out of the truth that we are but one of God's creatures.

A GUIDED REFLECTION ON THE ISSUES

Fact: To be humble you must know the Will of God and obey it.

Team leader

As a Team leader how can you show humility to individual members?

a. In the way you solve problems(choice of solutions)
b. In the way you communicate(choice of words)
c. In the way you negotiate(choice of terms)
d. In the way you keep your time(choice of time)

Team member

As a Team member how can you show humility to the leader?

a. In the way you solve problems(choice of solutions)
b. In the way you communicate(choice of words)
c. In the way you negotiate(choice of terms)
d. In the way you keep your time(choice of time)

Team member

As a Team member how can you show humility to customers?

a. In the way you solve problems(choice of solutions)
b. In the way you communicate(choice of words)
c. In the way you negotiate(choice of terms)
d. In the way you keep your time(choice of time)

VALUES IN THE WORKPLACE

2. Holiness In The Workplace

The workday includes the temptation to cross the line from what's holy to what's comfortable. The deep desire for acceptance can lead to compromised values and ethics.

How can I live out holiness with all the day-to-day pressures thrown at me in the workplace? One answer is to stay on course with God's purpose and plan for me. When I am overwhelmed and feel a surge of emotion flooding my body, I may have to escape and spend some time alone in the bathroom crying out to God to fill me with the fruits of His Spirit: love, joy, peace, patience, kindness, goodness, faithfulness, gentleness and self-control (Galatians 5:22–23).

Every day offers a challenge to live for Christ. Often the Holy Spirit's greatest work is teaching me to persist, to keep doing what is right even when it no longer seems interesting or exciting.

It's not just about doing right when something is obviously wrong. We need to focus on doing right when our duties become routine. This has been an ongoing lesson for me as I enter the 10th year with my current employer. It's easy to become complacent, and, therefore, become careless in making decisions that are not exciting and new. I have made some mistakes as a result of being comfortable — not demonstrating holiness and having to regain ground as a result.

God is in the marketplace 24/7 restoring, saving, redeeming and anointing me to rediscover His call on my life. The anointing for ministry was never meant just for church meetings. John 2:27 tells us the anointing we received from God abides in us. Wherever I go, His Spirit is powerfully

Worship God With your Work

available for me to demonstrate the gospel. My ministry platform may not be a pulpit or a small group but rather my business or vocation.

Serving Strategically
God is calling men and women of influence and power in the workplace to serve strategically for His purposes. We can't serve strategically without grasping a holy lifestyle — whether at home or work. We carry our lifestyle no matter where we are.

I started asking myself the following questions: What happens if I view my drive to work as an opportunity to pray for the day -for the decisions I will make, for my attitude and for those with whom I work? What happens if I pray "God, make my life and work stand out in ways that will lead people to ask questions"? What would happen if I actually viewed my workplace as a calling — an opportunity to reflect Christ not just through words but through my actions?

Living out holiness is not just about evangelizing. It's not about cramming Christian jargon down the throats of those with whom I come into contact. It's about relationships. It's about living like Jesus lived.

Relationships come with risk of rejection and hurt, but without risk, I cannot become the change agent God has called me to be. I know every day I have an opportunity to become part of someone's story. My story intersects with others each day.

One of my daily prayers is: "Lord, give me eyes to see and ears to hear what You need me to see and hear today." I need to pay attention to the intersections in my life. As my life has intersected with God, my life intersects with others to influence them. My story will become part of their story. How I interact with others and the wake I leave behind can make an eternal difference.

Worship God With your Work

Salt and Light
According to Matthew 5:13–14,
"You are the salt of the earth. ... You are the light of the world."

Both salt and light are agents of influence — not of power or control. This is a great reminder when I try to exercise servant leadership. It is not about control but enhancement — adding value to a situation or circumstance.

We all have influence in our workplace whether we are the CEO or a forklift driver. Our own example is the best way to introduce the good news.

At a place of employment, a warehouse worker sits in his car to read his Bible every day at lunchtime. He has had numerous opportunities to share because he first built a good reputation and demonstrated his values, people began to ask questions. He has handed out Bibles, and he now leads a Bible study for some of the warehouse workers.

Bringing people into God's kingdom is His work. Our responsibility is to be an available tool, allowing Him to use us and our story to change the ending of other stories.

So what does holiness look like? It's seeking the Holy Spirit to give you wisdom and guide you where He wants you to go. It's keeping your standards high, acting wisely and doing good whenever you can while having the fruits of the Spirit evident in your life. Whether at work, home or out with friends, we should be

"making the most of every opportunity, because the days are evil. Therefore do not be foolish, but understand what the Lord's will is" (Ephesians 5:16–17).

We are called to emulate His holiness in how we conduct our lives in the workplace. Let's follow Peter's advice:

Worship God With your Work

"Don't lazily slip back into those old grooves of evil, doing just what you feel like doing. You didn't know any better then; you do now. As obedient children, let yourselves be pulled into a way of life shaped by God's life, a life energetic and blazing with holiness. God said, 'I am holy; you be holy'" (I Peter 1:14–16 MSG).

Your workplace provides a great opportunity to practice holiness.

You were caught with earphones downloading and listening to music. Meanwhile you were supposed to be working on a big project.

Are you approaching your work with holiness? Here are some questions to help you evaluate:

- Do you work as unto the Lord—like He's your boss? By the way, that question applies whether you work in an office or as a stay-at-home mom.
- Are you diligent? Do you follow through on what you've been assigned?
- Why do you work? Do you have a hidden desire for recognition or human praise? Are you trying to impress people or to please the Lord?
- Do you treat other people fairly? Do you treat people the way God treats you?

No matter what's on your to-do list, remember Colossians 3:23:

"Whatever you do, work at it with all your heart, as working for the Lord, not for men."

Holiness is the trait of a Christ follower. Thus, holiness must be seen in all walks of our life. Another important aspect of life that often Christians do not live in holiness is at work places. Some Christians and very holy in the church, at times in the family but they are not at the work place. They argue that work place has got nothing to do with our faith and belief system. Work place is a 'worldly' thing that we are involved in which God is not concerned about.

Let us be reminded, a child of God remains a child of God and are required to live one standard lifestyle be it in church, home or at work places. So, as a Christian, we need to live a holy life even at our work place. People at work must see the differences in our speech and action. Christ must be portrayed in all our words and actions.

Paul in Ephesians 5: 5-8 admonishes the believers to bear a good testimony at work place. Do not be pretenders but be obedient and sincere in all that you do. The simple reason why we should shine at our work place is because we must first acknowledge that the vocation which we are in is God's calling for us.

If you are clerk at this point of time, you better be the best clerk in your office because we are the bondservant of Christ doing the will of God from the heart, with goodwill doing service, as to the Lord, and not to men (vs. 7-8). Remember!! By serving our earthly masters (bosses) faithfully and sincerely, we are actually rendering a faithful and acceptable service unto God.

Do not cheat at work place (undue Medical Leave, claims etc…). Do not abuse the office facilities (misusing the facilities for personal gain – telephone, Photostatting, printing etc..) God is dishonored when His children bears a poor testimony at work.

Holiness is all about living things the right way. In this context, it is living right and acceptable in the eyes of your bosses and of God.

A GUIDED REFLECTION ON THE ISSUES

Fact: To be holy you must know who you are and be who you are as a christian.

Team leader

As a Team leader how can you show holiness to individual members?

a. In the way you solve problems(choice of solutions)
b. In the way you communicate(choice of words)
c. In the way you negotiate(choice of terms)
d. In the way you keep your time(choice of time)

Team member

As a Team member how can you show holiness to the leader?

a. In the way you solve problems(choice of solutions)
b. In the way you communicate(choice of words)
c. In the way you negotiate(choice of terms)
d. In the way you keep your time(choice of time)

Team member

As a Team member how can you show holiness to customers?

a. In the way you solve problems(choice of solutions)
b. In the way you communicate(choice of words)
c. In the way you negotiate(choice of terms)
d. In the way you keep your time(choice of time)

VALUES IN THE WORKPLACE

3. Honesty In The Workplace

Dishonesty in the workplace takes two main forms- lying and stealing, and both are more common than many of us would like to think

Everyday examples of lying in the workplace include embellishing the truth on personal resumes and company track records; suggesting to customers that a product is better than it actually is; and promising bonuses to team members which never seem to arrive.

So deeply entrenched in business life are these practices, it seems only a brave or foolhardy person would go up against them. If everyone else is embellishing their resumes or company track records to get that job or contract, how can you not do the same?

If your competitors are selling a record number of products by promoting that product's not-so-true virtues, what are you meant to do – go broke telling the truth?

And how else can you motivate a disgruntled team member than by dangling a carrot which never gets any closer?

It's easy to say, "everyone else is doing it, so I'll do it, too." It's much harder to take an ethical stand and insist on honesty. But that is exactly what you must do if you want and expect honesty from your team members.

Surveys in America have conclusively proved that employees of any business tend to mimic the behavior- or perceived behavior – of the company's management.

Theft of cash, equipment, or company software is a serious

Worship God With your Work

crime and should be reported to the police, who will also advise on theft prevention strategies.

If management is prepared to distort the truth, bend the rules, or make undeliverable promises, why should team members do any differently?

If the boss thinks it's okay to raid the stationery locker every now and then, and take a couple of writing pads or a clutch of pens home to his kids, why should a sales clerk get into trouble for doing the same?

Nothing destroys morale among team members faster than "one rule for the boss, another rule for everyone else". With time people begin to question why they have to follow certain expectations when the boss doesn't.

But how do you stand tall and ask your team members to do the same when all around you, people seem to be lying, cheating, stealing, and doing anything else they think will put them ahead of the competition?

Case histories from human resource companies and business consultancies in America, Australia, and the United Kingdom suggest one good way would be to imagine the logical consequences of any action.

Embellishing your resume or company track record might not seem like such a big deal - until you realize how many people who rose to the top by this method also came crashing down when their lies were detected or it was discovered they couldn't actually do what they said they could.

Singing the praises of a product that doesn't make the grade may be quick route to short-term profit – but customers will eventually find out the product is no good and will lose faith in you.

Promising your team members bonuses you can't deliver might make them work harder in the short-term, but commerce is littered with the wreckage of companies which used that tactic.

If team members seem to be habitually lying in your business, that suggests having a good, hard look at your company rules. "Sometimes, unfair rules back people into corners," she told Kathy Thomas-Massey on an Inc.com website interview.

"If a company has a policy that penalizes people for staying home with their sick kids [for example], they're going to call in and lie about why they can't come to work. Fix the rules and you'll probably fix the problem."

And what about stealing? Australia-based Safety, Security and Manufacturing suggests one way to reduce the incidence of workplace theft is to increase employee awareness with educational programs.

"Make it clear that you won't tolerate theft and that employees will face discipline up to and including termination [if caught]. Let them know there are measures in place to detect theft," the organization says.

Such measures can include anything from improved inventory control to video surveillance. Of course, you need to distinguish between petty pilfering and major crime. If someone is nicking the odd batch of pens, you probably only need to remind them the pens are company property paid for by company funds – and make sure your own actions aren't inspiring a trend.

If you're not sure who the culprit is or have no real evidence with which to confront anyone, it's better to direct a general warning to all team members than to target any one person with suspicions.

A GUIDED REFLECTION ON THE ISSUES

Fact: To be honest you must know your calling(assignment) and fulfill your calling.

Team leader

As a Team leader how can you show honesty to individual members?

a. In the way you solve problems(choice of solutions)
b. In the way you communicate(choice of words)
c. In the way you negotiate(choice of terms)
d. In the way you keep your time(choice of time)

Team member

As a Team member how can you show honesty to the leader?

a. In the way you solve problems(choice of solutions)
b. In the way you communicate(choice of words)
c. In the way you negotiate(choice of terms)
d. In the way you keep your time(choice of time)

Team member

As a Team member how can you show honesty to customers?
a. In the way you solve problems(choice of solutions)
b. In the way you communicate(choice of words)
c. In the way you negotiate(choice of terms)
d. In the way you keep your time(choice of time)

VALUES IN THE WORKPLACE

4. Dependability In The Workplace

Dependability is a valuable quality in the workplace, whether it comes from your employees or vendors. Having a staff of dependable employees and managers helps your business run more smoothly and ensures that tasks are seen through to completion. An employee whom the boss can depend on is beneficial to the business, and a dependable employee has a greater possibility of seeing job growth and security.

Punctuality is an important component of dependability in the workplace. When an employee shows up late for work, especially on a regular basis, it can turn into a snowball effect including lateness to meetings and completing tasks after the deadline. Aside from arriving to work on time, a dependable employee completes projects within the time frame allotted. A repeated lack of timeliness on the part of an employee can cost your business money by turning off customers who have waited too long or by failing to deliver services or goods promised within a certain amount of time.

Productivity
Productive staff members help you achieve the business goals that further your business. A dependable employee can be counted on to do his portion of the work in a timely manner. Once finished with the job at hand, the same employee takes the initiative to speak with a supervisor or manager to find out what else can be done. Rather than spend extra time conducting personal business on the computer or telephone, a dependable, productive employee demonstrates team spirit by being willing to pitch in with other tasks once his task is completed.

Works Without Supervision
Time spent supervising employees prevents you from attending to your own work. Once an employee has completed

training necessary to doing the job, the ability to work independently helps build workplace trust and demonstrate the ability to handle other work. When an employee is dependable in the workplace, you don't have to check on him throughout the day to ensure work is being completed. This type of employee will take the initiative to get to work at the start of the workday, work independently and take breaks only when scheduled.

Attention to Detail
Your employees can be the eyes and ears of the company when you're not around. Dependable employees who pay attention to detail can catch mistakes that might cause the business to lose money or credibility. Being able to rely on employees to be your eyes and ears is an important part of quality assurance. Knowing you have employees whom you can trust to pay attention to the little details gives you the confidence to know the job is being done well, products are being made to your specifications and services of value are being offered to customers.

How to be a Dependable Employee
Being a dependable employee is a relatively easy process. If a person is committed to doing the best that they can in a workplace, they will be seen as dependable by most employers. Never making promises to deliver in many situations that they cannot is also very important. Making sure to always be on time for in meetings related to work is also a sign of dedication and dependable behavior. The majority of people are dependable if they understand that they need the position.

Many people stop being dependable in the workplace when they no longer feel appreciated within the work environment. A dependable person means that they understand that employees are expected to put their best foot forward whenever possible. A dependable employee will always be sure to be at work on time and positively achieve any objective set before them. This is being responsible both to oneself and to the employer. Everything that is expected of a dependable employee will be completed on time.

Dependable employees are always trying to solve problems within the company. They will always be available to share ideas and gives feedback about how to make the company better. They will often stay longer than the general workday if necessary and volunteer to be involved in strategy planning sessions to make the company more money when asked. They will spend extra time training new employees because they understand the value to having competent coworkers. They will not expect extra money for doing this, because they are grateful for the opportunity to have regular employment.

Dependable workers are always willing to learn new skills if they will benefit the company. Expanding education is something that they are willing to do because they want to be viewed as successful contributors to the company as a whole. It is important for these people to be viewed well. They tend to be very diplomatic when dealing with other employees. This is because they understand that not working well as a team will not result in regular improvements for the company.

A dependable person will never abuse sick time, or take vacation when it will be detrimental to the financial success of the company. The more people are willing to appreciate how dependable a person is, the more dependable they will become. Compliments are the best reward for a dependable employee. Dependable employees sometimes also encourage others in the office to work to a higher standard. This is because they receive a high level of respect from others in the workplace.

Do you want to be a dependable employee?
I think to some degree that everyone wants to be an employee that can be relied upon to do a good job, but what does it really take to be a dependable employee? It is really easy to

be reliable, but to be dependable takes a new level of talent and motivation to your craft. So what does it take to be a dependable employee?

The first thing you need to have is the trust and confidence of your co-workers. So people can rely on you to get to work, so what? Can you do a good job when you get there? Do people have faith that you are going to show up and do a good job, or are they hoping that you don't show up so the job can get done faster? People can't depend on those who don't do a good job.

Being dependable means you can take instructions and orders from others and work as a team with other people. When people can depend on you that means that they know that you are going to be a team player and not always be about yourself. If someone needs a hand, you can be counted on to give that person a hand. When someone needs you to stay late, you will stay late without whining about it.

A dependable employee can also work in independent situations as well. Being dependable means that you could be put in the middle of a cornfield and you are going to get your work done regardless of any distractions that might be put forth. The company can trust that the reports will be done and you won't spend your whole day on the Internet researching sports scores.

When you are labeling an employee as someone who is dependable, you are talking about someone who can do the job without you having to worry about that person. What this means is that the assignment will get done without a lot of delay or stopping to figure out what to do. That employee will be able to use the knowledge that they have to good use.

Are you a dependable employee? Can you work as part of a team, or by yourself, without a lot of fuss? Can you get the job that you are assigned to do done without too many delays? If this is you, then you are a dependable employee that any company would love to have on the team.

If you are interested in turning your internship into a job offer, it's important to know exactly what employers look for when hiring full-time employees. In addition to relevant skills, employers seek employees who have the personal values, characteristics, and personality traits that spell success. Good personal values are what makes the foundation for a good employee. Internships are an excellent time to show employers that you have the personal traits that they value in their employees.

Do not make the mistake of missing the opportunity to show your supervisors at your internship that you have what it takes to be successful on the job as well as possessing the personal characteristics they value. An internship is an opportunity to learn the skills and behaviors along with the work values that are required for success in the workplace.

A GUIDED REFLECTION ON THE ISSUES

Fact: To be dependable you must renew your mind.

Team leader

As a Team leader how can you show dependability to individual members?

a. In the way you solve problems(choice of solutions)
b. In the way you communicate(choice of words)
c. In the way you negotiate(choice of terms)
d. In the way you keep your time(choice of time)

Team member

As a Team member how can you show dependability to the leader?

a. In the way you solve problems(choice of solutions)
b. In the way you communicate(choice of words)
c. In the way you negotiate(choice of terms)
d. In the way you keep your time(choice of time)

Team member

As a Team member how can you show dependability to customers?

a. In the way you solve problems(choice of solutions)
b. In the way you communicate(choice of words)
c. In the way you negotiate(choice of terms)
d. In the way you keep your time(choice of time)

VALUES IN THE WORKPLACE

5. Benevolence In The Workplace

"This is the ultimate key to business success." Senior Mananger, Nokia Academy Global "What we all need to know. I've been sharing this with everyone." Senior Information Officer, World Bank In the vast majority of businesses, the expression People are our most important asset is little more than a plaque on the wall.

The organizations that have actually put this principle to work, however, have demonstrated a consistent advantage over their competitors in the areas of employee retention, innovation, productivity, and profitability. Management experts are finally realizing that the development of human resources will be the key to business success in the foreseeable future, and in the words of one reader, Real Love in the Workplace is the only book that explains what every person in the workplace needs most, as well as what we can do to provide it.

We are all instinctively aware that every human being has a primal need for love, but most of us fail to realize that this need continues into the workplace for every manager, direct report, CEO, vendor, consultant, board member, co-worker, and customer. If we don t address that primal need, all our attempts to optimize business indicators productivity and profitability, for example will be frustrated to a significant degree. If we do address that uniquely human need if we do what s necessary to produce happy employees, managers, and customers profits will naturally follow. In Real Love in the Workplace, you will learn

1. How to become the kind of leader people will want to follow.
2. How to create customers who are not just satisfied but eager to stay with your company.

Worship God With your Work

3. How to create a work environment where employees are communicative, creative, cooperative, and happy.
4. How to eliminate not just manage conflict in the workplace.
5. How to correct behaviors in a way that people will be eager to hear it.

Don't be afraid of love in the workplace
Mention love at the office and minds go to tawdry affairs, lines crossed and calls to human resources.

People see love as a squishy emotion, one that breeds conflict, a distraction. So it has largely been drummed out of the workplace.
That's a shame. Focus on the pitfalls of romantic love and you'll miss the importance of love's broader meaning: kindness; respect; empathy.

With that in mind, and in the words of famed workplace expert Celine Dion, let's talk about love.

Companies are undoubtedly trending toward more compassionate cultures, but there has been little recognition in professional or academic circles about how central love is to a truly caring work environment.

Sigal Barsade, a management professor at the University of Pennsylvania's Wharton School, and Olivia O'Neill, an assistant professor of management at George Mason University, have conducted a study that shows how "a culture of companionate love" is good for employees and clients.

The study defines compassionate love as the sense of warmth, affection and the friendly connections that bind us. Barsade said she believes our inability to separate the idea of passionate love from companionate love is the reason love is so often overlooked in the workplace.

"Within the management domain, the word 'love' evokes this concept of this soft, fuzzy thing that you really can't take seriously at work," she said. "But compassionate love is one of the basic emotions of human experience. Given how much time we spend at work, it's actually ignorant to think it wouldn't be a part of our work lives."

The longitudinal study, which will be published in an upcoming edition of the journal Administrative Science Quarterly, surveyed patients, their family members, and workers at a long-term health care facility. Employees who felt they worked in a "culture of compassionate love" had less absenteeism, were better at teamwork, were more satisfied with their jobs and experienced lower levels of emotional exhaustion. In turn, the facility's clients and their families were happier with the service they received.

The researchers did a follow-up survey of 3,201 workers in seven industries, just to show that the results weren't specific to the health care field. Barsade and O'Neill wrote in a recent post on the Harvard Business Review's website: "People who worked in a culture where they felt free to express affection, tenderness, caring, and compassion for one another were more satisfied with their jobs, committed to the organization, and accountable for their performance."

This all seems rather sensible. So I asked Barsade: Why don't companies just do this anyway?

She said management literature from the early 1900s to the late 1930s does discuss "the concept of love and caring as part of work."

"But I think people's perspective on what kind of emotions mattered at work, if they mattered at all, narrowed in World War II as the focus became more, 'How do we keep people satisfied?'" Barsade said. "Emotion turned into satisfaction, and that changed the focus to wages and how the job is designed. Emotion somehow was either ignored or became illegitimate. We started thinking that people shouldn't have emotions at work, and if they do, they should be repressed."

The study cites two examples, one of a workplace with a strong culture of compassionate love, the other without. In the first, an employee is quoted as saying: "We are a family. When you walk in the door, you can feel it. Everyone cares for each other regardless of whatever level you are in. We all watch out for each other."

In the second, a veteran employee of 30 years tells her supervisor that her mother-in-law has died, and the supervisor responds by bluntly saying: "I have staff that handles this. I don't want to deal with it."

That's a sizable difference, and it's easy to see which workplace is going to have more loyal and motivated workers.

So if your workplace lacks compassionate love, how did you improve?

Barsade said some of it can be mandated: "For example, say you're a manager and you get copied on an email chain between two employees that's not civil. And you got to them and say: 'This is not acceptable here. We don't speak to each other that way.' I actually think we can be a lot more explicit about what our norms are, about how we interact with one another."

Of course, a change in culture has to not only be dictated by those in charge, it has to be demonstrated by them as well. Bosses can provide employees with flexibility, pay them well and show them they are trusted and valued. They can also — and here we get into my mantra again — behave like decent human beings.

"Management has to show it too," Barsade said. "Not just structurally, but through their own facial expressions, body language and behavior. People show love at work because they feel it. It becomes a normative expectation that this is how you behave here."

This doesn't mean we spend the day hugging and gently consoling people when they screw up. Rules and ethics can stand on equal footing with a culture of compassionate love — we respect and care for each other AND we follow the rules of the company.

I can see some writing this off as too sappy for the hard-knock world of business. If that's what you think, consider how much better you function when you feel cared for and supported.

Then imagine if that sense of love didn't have to stay home when you leave for work each day.

A GUIDED REFLECTION ON THE ISSUES

Fact: To be benevolent you must help others.

Team leader

As a Team leader how can you show benevolence to individual members?

a. In the way you solve problems(choice of solutions)
b. In the way you communicate(choice of words)
c. In the way you negotiate(choice of terms)
d. In the way you keep your time(choice of time)

Team member

As a Team member how can you show benevolence to the leader?

a. In the way you solve problems(choice of solutions)
b. In the way you communicate(choice of words)
c. In the way you negotiate(choice of terms)
d. In the way you keep your time(choice of time)

Team member

As a Team member how can you show benevolence to customers?

a. In the way you solve problems(choice of solutions)
b. In the way you communicate(choice of words)
c. In the way you negotiate(choice of terms)
d. In the way you keep your time(choice of time)

Worship God With your Work

PSALMS, HYMNS AND SPIRITUAL SONGS

1. NO KING BUT JESUS
Every kingdom trembles, trembles
Every power crumbles, crumbles
When the name of Jesus is mentioned in faith
Every knee bows in worship to the king of Kings

Chorus
There is no king but King Jesus
We proclaim Him the only king
He's exalted, highly exalted
Far above kingdoms and thrones

Bridge
Dominion, glory and a kingdom
The father has bestowed on the Son
Jesus, Jesus Jesus
All nations shall serve you

2. BY THE BLOOD
By the blood of Jesus Christ
We are washed and sanctified
Created anew by the Spirit of God
Who works in us both to will
Will and to do
What He wants us to do

Chorus
In Him we live
And move and have our being
Father we are your workmanship
Created for good works
And for your pleasure Lord
We are and were created

3. MY WILL DOESN'T MATTER
I present my body
As a living sacrifice
Holy and acceptable to you Oh Lord
Order my steps
Moment by moment
To bring glory to your name

Chorus
My Will doesn't matter anymore
I've laid it down to do your Will
All the days l live
Willingly, joyfully, sincerely
I yield to you
Use me as you will

Bridge
Use me, use me, use me as you will (Lord)
Use me, use me, use me as you will.

4. SEE THE LORD
See the Lord Jesus Christ
See the King of glory on His throne
See the host of angels hail the King
Bowing before His throne

Chorus
Make His praises glorious
Oh lift your voices and join the angels
Make His praises glorious
Let everything that has breath praise the Lord

Make His praises glorious
from shore to shore
Till His glory fills the earth

5. GLORIFY
Glorify, magnify
Oh exalt Jesus Christ the Lord
He is worthy of all our praise
Let everything that has breath
Praise the Lord

Chorus
Oh who is like our God in power?
Oh who is like our God in wisdom?
Oh who is like our God in splendor?
He's above all, far above all
We worship, honour and hallow you
Oh Jesus Christ

6. YOU HAVE MADE US
You died for us to live
To live as God's children
We just cannot cease lifting holy hands
Lifting psalms and hymns and spiritual songs
To you our God and King

Chorus
You have made us
And not we ourselves
We are the sheep of your pasture
All that we are
And hope to be
We owe it all to you

7. IN YOUR PRESENCE
As I come into your presence
And leave the world behind me
Alone with you oh Lord
Gazing at your glory
My soul receives strength
Everything becomes possible
Oh Lord how I love your presence

Chorus
In your presence Oh Lord
There is fullness of joy
And all impossibilities become possible
In your presence Oh Lord
There is fullness of joy
Everything that is dead in us
Begins to live again

Bridge
Thou Oh Lord will keep in perfect peace
He whose mind is stayed on you
Thou Oh God will keep in perfect peace
He whose mine is stayed on you

8. I LIVE
Great is the mystery of godliness
We have this treasure in earthen vessels
That the excellency of the power
May be of God
As we triumph over the flesh
And reign in life
By the faith of the Son of God.

Worship God With your Work

Chorus
I live but it's not I
It's Christ who lives in me 2x
He's changing me from glory to glory
From glory to glory
He's changing me from glory to glory
into His image.

9. JESUS OH JESUS
You humbled yourself
To be born in a manger
And to be raised by a carpenter
You left your glory above
You came down to die for man
Now oh Lord you are exalted
Over all principalities

Chorus
Jesus oh Jesus Christ 2x
Your name is higher than all names
Jesus Christ you are Lord
Your name is higher than all names
Jesus Christ you are Lord

Bridge
Lord of Lords
You are Lord of Lords 2x
Head of all principalities and powers

10. SO I WILL GLORIFY
In your presence
Demons flee
In your presence
Yokes are broken
Limitations are removed
Prisoners are released
In your presence

Chorus
So I will glorify your name
I will magnify your name
Oh Lord forever, to live forever
in your presence
For you dwell in the praises of
you people

Bridge
Keep me always in your presence
I delight in you
There is nothing I desire on earth
besides you Lord
I love to be with you
I love to be where you are
I love your presence Lord

OTHER BOOKS BY THE AUTHOUR

WHILST THE DEW IS ON THE ROSES

This is a 129-page inspiring book which recounts how we show forth the praises of God as members of His body by exercising, discharging or delivering our royal mandate through Praise, Worship and Prayer till enemies are made His footstool.

The authour underlines the importance of this to our prosperity and protection as children of God and recommends the first fruits of our day i.e. the early hours, to be devoted to fellowship with God, lift up praise, lift up worship and lift up prayer to:

-show forth the praise of God.
But ye are a chosen generation, a royal priesthood, a holy nation, a peculiar people, that ye should show forth the praises of Him who hath called you out of darkness into His marvelous light. 1 Pt. 2:9.

-bring His enemies under His feet
Then cometh the end, when he shall have delivered up the kingdom to God, even the Father; when he shall have put down all rule and all authority and power. For he must reign, till he hath put all enemies under his feet. The last enemy that shall be destroyed is death. 1 Cor. 15:24-26

-keep the adversary constantly on the retreat
I will build my church, and the gates of hell shall not prevail against it. I will give you the keys of the kingdom of heaven, and whatever you bind on earth shall be bound in heaven, and whatever you loose on earth shall be loosed in heaven. Matt. 16:18-19.

We are a royal priesthood and that denotes our royal and priesthood mandates are inextricably linked. Furthermore it goes without saying that the priesthood anointing, daily renewed through waiting on God (Praise, Worship and Prayer) is the source of our strength as Kings and Priests.

And hast made us unto our God kings and priests: and we shall reign on the earth. Rev. 5:10.

G.O.A.L.S PRINCIPLE

G.O.A.L.S Principle is an 84-page book that promotes Christian Values at home, School and the Workplace- shows how these Values are developed and how they influence our goals, daily choices and decisions to lead lives pleasing to God, just like Jesus Christ did.

The authour educates you on your divine purpose and inspires you to rise above your personal challenges and impact your immediate environment and beyond.

The release of this book is long overdue. The need for every new convert that joins the local Church to have a copy cannot be overemphasized.

It should also be a helpful resource material for schools and all stakeholder institutions in personal and spiritual development of young people.

Parents especially, should have copies of this tool in their tool boxes because they have the fundamental and awesome responsibility to ensure that their children grow up in the knowledge and fear of God to come into the fullness of the image and likeness of Jesus Christ, the Son of God. Prov. 22:6.

WALKING IN HIS STEPS

This is an inspiring 89-page book which sheds light on self leadership and it is the conviction of the author that with book, your situation cannot be worse, it can only be better- for Christ in you is the hope of glory. Good success in life depends on godly self-leadership and godly self leadership depends on how we answer the following questions:

1. Who am I? (NEW CREATION- be born again)
2. Where am I going? (DESTINY- become like Christ)
3. How can I get there? (DISCIPLESHIP- walk in His steps)

Waling In His Steps empowers you to show leadership for your personal life (plan and manage your life) by exhibiting the following godly qualities:

1. Humility- be godly (recognize and respect the Bible as you plan and manage your life)

2. Holiness -master sin (rise above temptations and trials)

3. Honesty-examine your life daily(look into the perfect law of liberty daily)

4. Dependability-live from a position of victory(your mission is achievable)

5. Benevolence- impact your immediate environment and beyond(bring up others to your level)

www.ingramcontent.com/pod-product-compliance
Lightning Source LLC
Chambersburg PA
CBHW071758170526
45167CB00003B/1084